HEY GUY, ARE YOU:

A) GETTING OLDER?
B) GETTING BETTER?
C) GETTING BALDER?

CARTOONS BY: Vincent Andriani

WRITTEN BY: Lee Ann Ahern, Bill Bridgeman, Bill Gray, Marn Jensen, Kevin Kinzer, Mark Oatman, Dan Taylor, Rich Warwick, and Myra Zirkle.

WHEN YOU HAVE TROUBLE FALLING ASLEEP, YOU ATTEMPT TO INDUCE DROWSINESS BY:

A. DRINKING WARM MILK.

B. READING A BOOK.

C. COUNTING THE NUMBER OF PAIN RELIEF MEDICATIONS YOU TOOK THAT DAY.

THE PHYSICAL FEATURE YOU'RE BEST KNOWN FOR IS:

A) YOUR WARM AND WINNING SMILE.

B) YOUR PLAYFUL, TWINKLING EYES.

C) HAIR CIRCLED OVER YOUR BALD SPOT LIKE A COILED ROPE.

(back view)

WHAT DO YOU SEE IN THIS INK BLOT?

A) ARTIFICIAL HEART.

B) HOOD ORNAMENT OF '37 HUDSON.
   (Now <u>that</u> was a car!)

C) ATTRACTIVE WOMAN.

THE LAST THING YOU DO BEFORE GOING TO BED AT NIGHT IS:

A) BRUSH YOUR TEETH.

B) OPEN THE WINDOW.

C) WATCH THE SIX O'CLOCK NEWS.

8.

RIDDLE: HOW MANY GUYS YOUR AGE DOES IT TAKE TO SCREW IN A LIGHT BULB?

ANSWER: JUST ONE.
THE PROBLEM IS GETTING HIM UP AND DOWN THE LADDER.

THE MOST IMPORTANT QUALITIES YOU LOOK FOR IN A WOMAN ARE:

A) A GREAT FIGURE AND A LUSTY SEXUAL APPETITE.

B) STUNNING GOOD LOOKS AND A TASTE FOR ADVENTURE.

C) POOR EYESIGHT AND A LACK OF STANDARDS.

10.

YOUR FAVORITE SOURCE OF CURRENT EVENTS IS:

A) WATCHING TV NEWS SPECIALS.

B) READING NEWSPAPER EDITORIALS.

C) PEERING OUT THE WINDOW.

"STANDARD EQUIPMENT"

ON ANY CAR YOU'D CONSIDER BUYING WOULD BE:

A) A QUALITY STEREO.

B) AN ELECTRIC WINDOW DEFOGGER.

C) A DASHBOARD COMPASS AND THICK PLASTIC SEAT COVERS.

NAME THIS PICTURE --

A) A VERY BROKEN NECKLACE.

B) A ROW OF BOULDERS.

C) AN AERIAL VIEW OF A GUY YOUR AGE HOLDING UP TRAFFIC.

WHEN YOU HEAR THE SONG "BRIDGE OVER TROUBLED WATER" YOU IMMEDIATELY THINK OF:

A) THE TURBULENT SIXTIES.

B) A POPULAR SINGING DUO.

C) DENTURES IN A DIRTY GLASS.

A) STAR WARS.

B) CASABLANCA.

C) SILENT.

19.

DO YOU OWN TWO OR MORE OF THE FOLLOWING AUTO ACCESSORIES?

A) TENNIS BALL ON TRAILER HITCH.

B) CURB FEELERS.

C) AUTO COMPASS.

D) FELT HAT.

E) SPEEDOMETER THAT ONLY GOES TO 45 MPH.

YOU WEAR YOUR HAIR:

A) LONG.

B) SHORT.

C) WHEN YOU CAN REMEMBER.

THE MOST ENJOYABLE ASPECT OF HAVING A NICE LAWN IS:

A) THE VISUAL PLEASURE IT GIVES.

B) COMPLIMENTS FROM THE NEIGHBORS.

C) CRITICIZING THE YARD WORK BEFORE YOU PAY THE KID.

DO YOU KNOW WHAT THIS IS ?

(YOUR WINDOWS AS SEEN AFTER 8:00 p.m.)

23.

WHAT DOES THIS SILHOUETTE MOST CLOSELY RESEMBLE?

A) BRONTOSAURUS, A VEGETARIAN WITH A SMALL BRAIN.

B) TYRANNOSAURUS, A MEAT-EATER TRAPPED IN THE ICE AGE.

C) "SKIPPY," YOUR FIRST PET AND BEST FRIEND.

24.

SOMEDAY YOU HOPE TO:

A)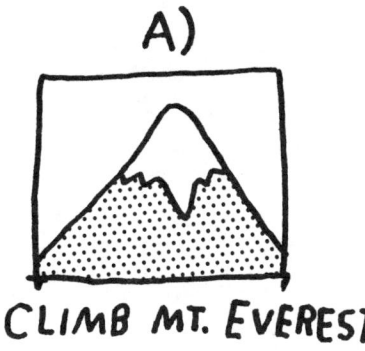
CLIMB MT. EVEREST.

B)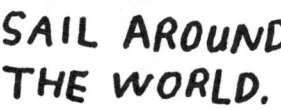
SAIL AROUND THE WORLD.

C)
DO A PUSH-UP.

STORY PROBLEM

IF YOU AND ANOTHER CAR START AT POINT A, AND YOU'RE DRIVING AT 19 MPH AND THE OTHER CAR IS TRAVELING AT 17 MPH, WHICH OF YOU WILL ARRIVE FIRST AT POINT B, FIVE MILES AWAY?

ANSWER <u>THE OTHER CAR.</u> PEOPLE YOUR AGE ALWAYS <u>SLOW WAY DOWN</u> AT THE INTERSECTIONS.

26.

YOUR IDEA OF A ROMANTIC EVENING INCLUDES:

A) Champagne, caviar and passionate lovemaking.

B) Fine wine, imported cheese and passionate lovemaking.

C) Prune juice, soda crackers and an apology.

WHEN YOU SEE "PUNKS" WHO HAVE MOHAWK HAIRDOS, YOU THINK:

A) THEY MUST BE REBELLING AGAINST SOCIETY.

B) THEY MUST VALUE SELF-EXPRESSION.

C) THEY MUST HAVE HAIR TO BURN. (CURSE THEM!)

DO YOU HAVE 2 OR MORE OF THE FOLLOWING BUMPER STICKERS ON YOUR CAR?

> DON'T BLAME ME... I VOTED FOR HOOVER!

> IF YOU CAN READ THIS PLEASE TELL ME WHAT IT SAYS.

> IF THIS VAN'S A-ROCKIN', GET THE ALIGNMENT CHECKED.

> MY OTHER CAR IS A THREE-WHEELED BIKE.

> GOUT HAPPENS.

> HONK IF YOU'RE... OH FORGET IT, I'LL NEVER HEAR YOU.

YOU THINK THE STONES ARE:

A) A ROCK GROUP.

B) A LEGEND IN THEIR OWN TIME.

C) REALLY MESSING UP YOUR KIDNEYS.

"OUT FOR THE EVENING" PROBABLY REFERS TO YOUR:

A) ENJOYMENT OF CULTURAL EVENTS.

B) INTEREST IN STRENUOUS EXERCISE.

C) 3rd AND 5th VERTEBRAE.

31.

WHICH OF THESE DOESN'T BELONG?

1. HAIR DYE

2. BODY BUILDER

3. ANTACID

4. DENTURE CREAM

TRICK QUESTION -- THEY ALL BELONG. (YOU NEED THE BODY BUILDER TO OPEN THEM FOR YOU.)

RIDDLE: WHY DID A GUY YOUR AGE CROSS THE ROAD?

Because he was on his way to the bank during the noon rush to pay all his bills, balance his checking account and deposit twenty dollars worth of pennies, each of which has a personal history that he will want to share with a teller.

WHAT IS THIS PICTURE?

A) AN INSTRUMENT OF TORTURE.

B) THE LETTER "E" LYING ON ITS BACK.

C) ALL THE COMB YOU'LL EVER NEED.

A TWO-PART READING COMPREHENSION TEST

READ THE FOLLOWING PARAGRAPHS AND PAY ATTENTION TO DETAIL SO THAT YOU CAN ANSWER THE QUESTIONS WITHOUT LOOKING BACK.

PART ONE...

OUR FRIEND THE CANE.

CANES COME IN A VARIETY OF SHAPES AND SIZES. THEY CAN BE AN ATTRACTIVE ADDITION TO ANY OUTFIT AND ARE QUITE HELPFUL WHEN FACING A CHALLENGE LIKE A CURB. THEY ARE ALSO GOOD FOR SHAKING AT ANYONE BORN AFTER THE BIG WAR AND YELLING "YOUNG PUNKS!" YES, THE CANE IS TRULY A TRUSTY FRIEND.

THE MAIN THEME OF THIS PARAGRAPH IS:

A) THE CANE CAN BE A USEFUL TOOL.

B) THE CANE IS OUR FRIEND.

C) "YOUNG PUNKS! YOUNG PUNKS!"

PART TWO...

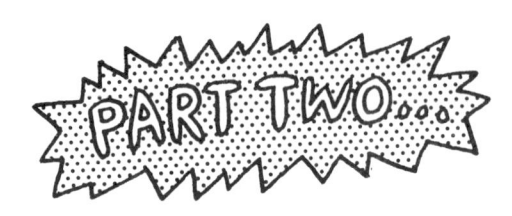

A VISIT TO CANADA

CANADA IS OUR NEIGHBOR TO THE NORTH. IT IS KNOWN FOR ITS INTERESTING PEOPLE, WINTER SPORTS AND MOUNTED POLICE. THE PEOPLE OF CANADA ARE CALLED "CANADIANS." IF YOU GET A CHANCE TO VISIT CANADA, YOU SHOULD.

THE MAIN THEME OF THIS PARAGRAPH IS:

A) CANADA WOULD MAKE A GOOD VACATION SPOT.

B) CANADA IS VERY INTERESTING.

C) "YOUNG PUNKS! YOUNG PUNKS!"

Whenever you see a picture of a cow:

A) YOU ARE OVERWHELMED WITH GRATITUDE FOR THE GIFTS IT GIVES.

B) YOU ARE REMINDED OF A SIMPLER LIFE, A SIMPLER TIME.

C) YOU RESENT IT BECAUSE IT GETS TO LICK SALT.

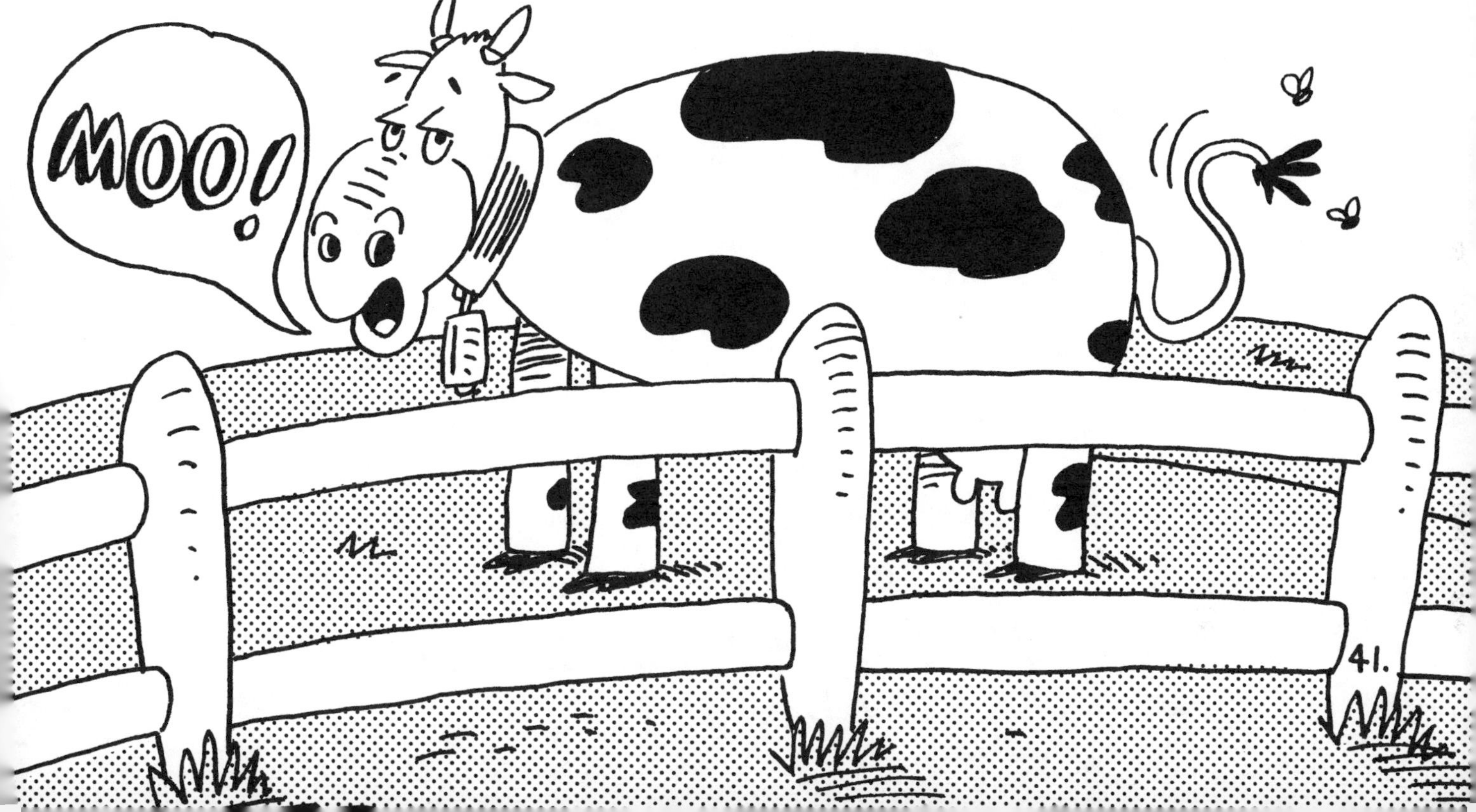
MOO!
41.

YOUR SLEEPWEAR IS:

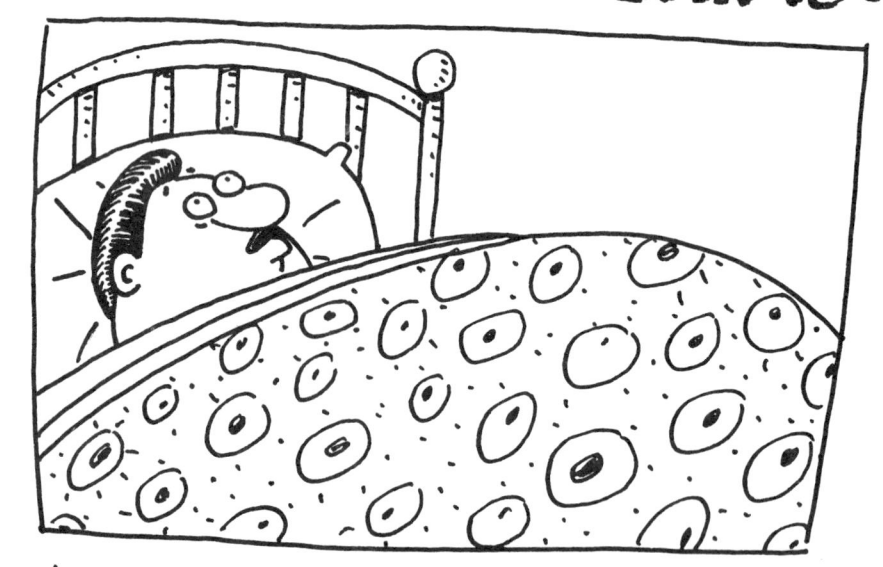

A) BRIEF AND PROVOCATIVE.
B) DESIGNED FOR COMFORT.
C) A MAZE OF HEATING COILS AND TRACTION DEVICES.

WHAT DO YOU SEE IN THIS PICTURE?

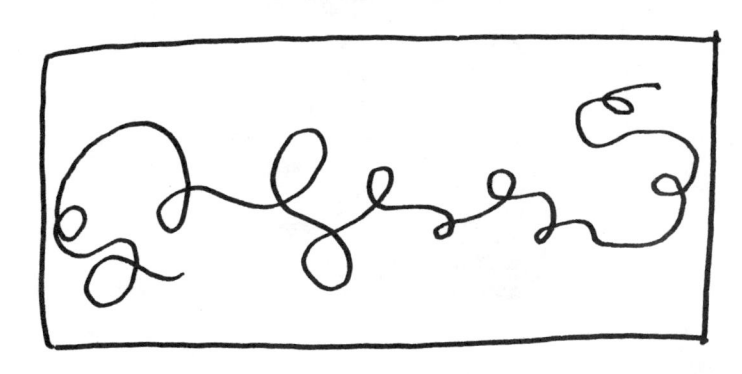

A) ROUTE NORMALLY TAKEN TO BATHROOM.

B) SHOELACE YOU TIED ALL BY YOURSELF.

C) CURRENT SIGNATURE.

43.

AS YOU GET OLDER, IT GETS MORE AND MORE OBVIOUS THAT _____ IS A **COMMIE PLOT**.
(fill in blank)

A) DÉTENTE.

B) SKATEBOARDING.

C) PRETTY MUCH EVERYTHING.

44.

LET's PLAY CONNECT THE DOTS!

45.

THE TRENDY "CATCH PHRASE" YOUR FRIENDS KNOW YOU BY IS:

A) "What's up?"

B) "What's happenin'?"

C) "What?"

46.

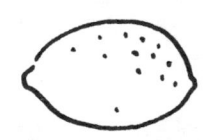

WHEN LIFE HANDS YOU LEMONS, YOU:

A) MAKE LEMONADE.

B) MAKE WHISKEY SOURS.

C) EAT THE PEEL AS A SOURCE OF FIBER.

YOU RECOGNIZE THIS SYMBOL AS:

A) ROCK AND ROLL -- THAT DARN MUSIC THAT SCARES YOUR CAT.

B) REST AND RELAXATION -- YOUR TWO FAVORITE HOBBIES.

C) BIG TRAIN WITHIN STATE BOUNDARIES -- STOP AND BLOCK TRAFFIC ON THE OFF-CHANCE IT MIGHT SHOW UP.

48.

YOU REMEMBER 1984 AS:

A) A BANNER YEAR FOR THE STOCK MARKET.

B) A CLASSIC WORK OF LITERATURE.

C) THE LAST TIME YOU HAD SEX.

WHAT DO YOU SEE IN THE FOLLOWING SCENE?

A) THE CAREFREE WORLD OF CHILDREN.
B) ENERGY AND VITALITY.
C) A BUNCH OF SMART ALECK WHIPPERSNAPPERS WHO ARE PROBABLY UP TO NO GOOD.

AT YOUR BIRTHDAY PARTY, FRIENDS AND FAMILY WILL SING:

A) "HAPPY BIRTHDAY TO YOU."

B) "AULD LANG SYNE."

C) "WHOLE LOTTA SHAKIN' GOIN' ON."

WHAT'S WRONG WITH THIS PICTURE?

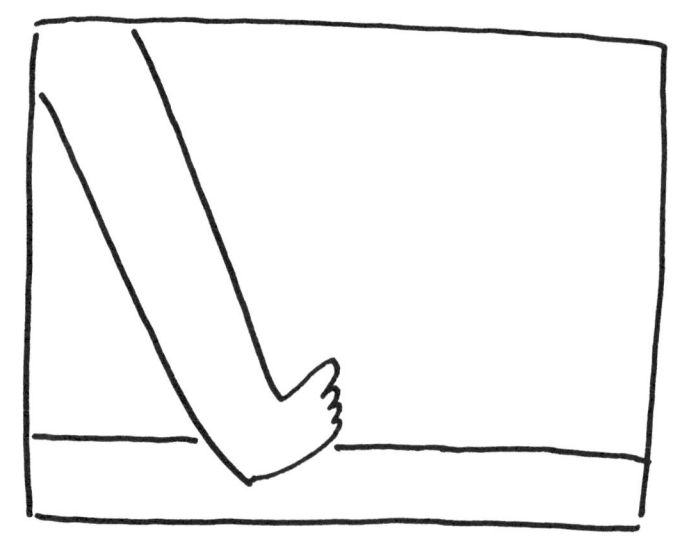

A) IT'S NOT VERY WELL DRAWN.

B) IT DOESN'T SHOW ENOUGH VEIN.

C) WHERE ARE THE ELASTIC BANDAGES?

YOU WOULD RATHER TAKE:

A) FIRST PLACE IN A MARATHON.

B) FIRST PLACE IN A TRIATHLON.

C) A NAP.

"MALL-WALKING" IS:

A) A GREAT FORM OF ALL-WEATHER EXERCISE.

B) A FUN WAY TO MEET NEW PEOPLE.

C) A CLEVER WAY TO HIDE THE FACT YOU'VE FORGOTTEN WHAT YOU CAME TO BUY.

55.

YOUR FAVORITE PARTY GAME IS:

A) HIDE AND GO SLEEP.

B) DOCTOR, MAY I?

C) PIN THE BLAME ON THE GOVERNMENT.

56.

YOU THOUGHT THE MOVIE "FATAL ATTRACTION" WAS:

A) SOCIALLY RELEVANT.

B) AN UNFAIR PORTRAYAL OF SINGLE WOMEN.

C) ABOUT AN OLD GUY BUYING A BURRITO.

57.

OBVIOUSLY A ROAD SIGN IN THIS SHAPE SIGNIFIES:

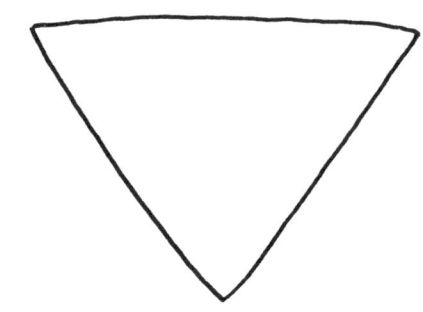

▽

A) INVERTED PYRAMID AHEAD.

B) CHEWABLE ANTACIDS AHEAD.

C) SLOW DOWN. (ALL ROAD SIGNS MEAN SLOW DOWN.)

STORY PROBLEM

IF YOU'RE PUSHING YOUR GROCERY CART DOWN THE MIDDLE OF THE AISLE AND SOMEONE ELSE YOUR AGE IS HEADED TOWARD YOU, ALSO PUSHING HIS CART DOWN THE MIDDLE OF THE AISLE, AT WHAT POINT WILL A COLLISION OCCUR?

ANSWER: THERE WILL BE NO COLLISION. YOU WILL STOP NEXT TO EACH OTHER, THEREFORE BLOCKING THE ENTIRE AISLE.

WHICH ARE YOUR TEETH?

TRUE OR FALSE?

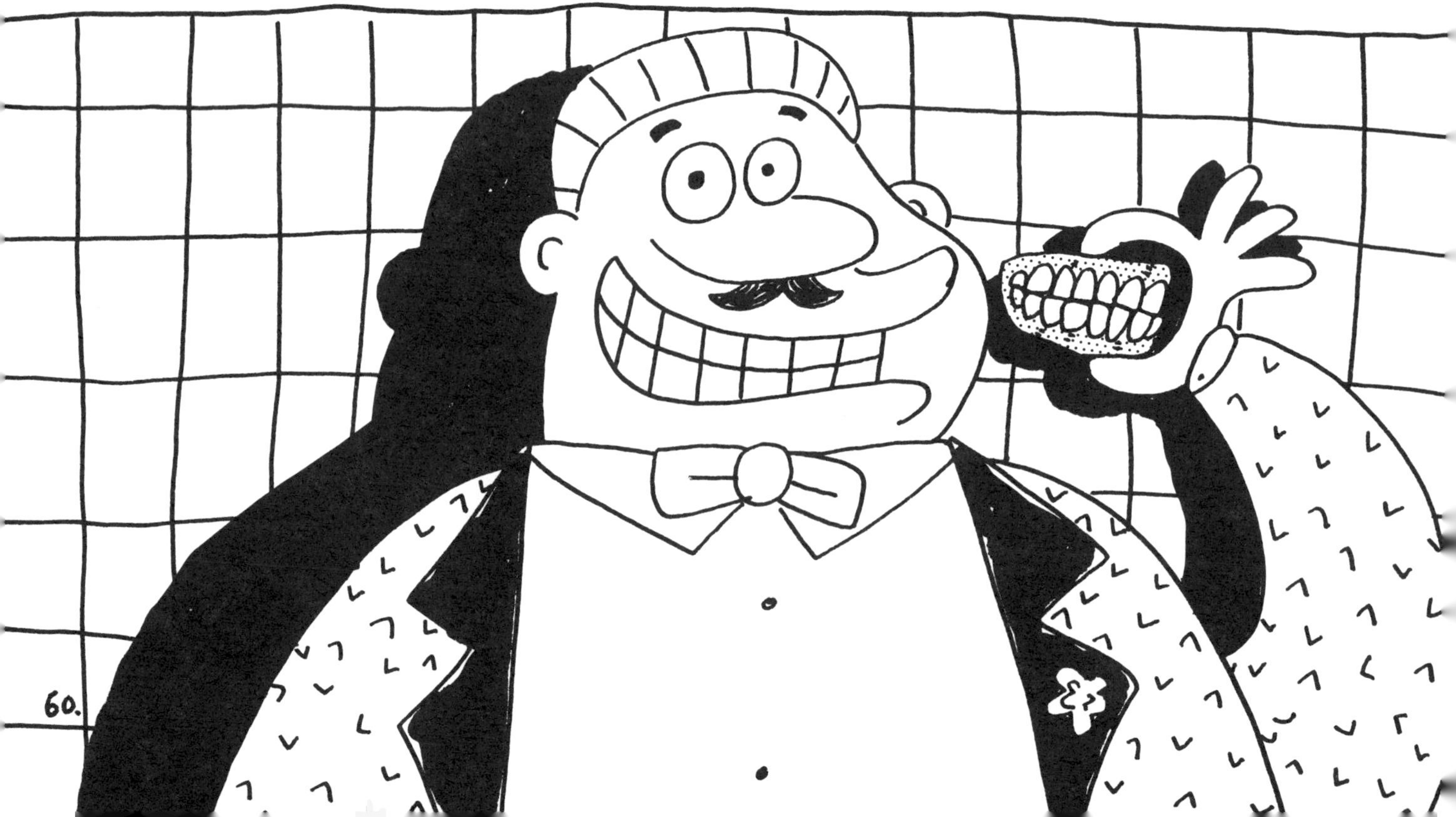

THE PHRASE "HELL NO, WE WON'T GO!" IS:

A) A PHRASE FROM 1960'S PROTEST MARCHES.

B) HOW YOUR KIDS FEEL ABOUT SCHOOL.

C) SOMETHING FOLKS YOUR AGE SAY A LOT.

61.

HOW MANY OF THESE OLD HIT TUNES DO YOU RECOGNIZE?

1. "ROCKER 'ROUND THE CLOCK."

2. "PRUNE RIVER."

3. "SLEEPIN' ON A JET PLANE."

4. "LET ME BE."

DO YOU KNOW WHAT THIS IS?

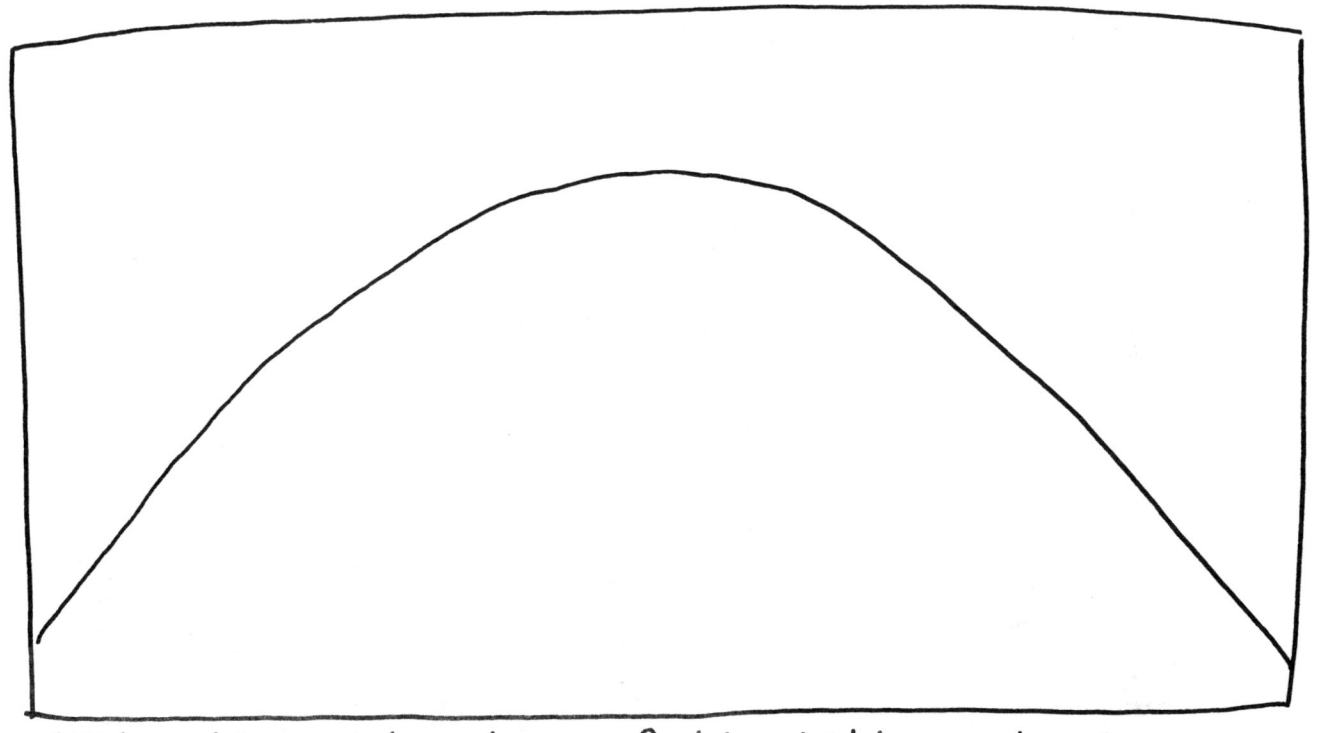

(It's the side view of the hill you just went over.)

63.

YOU THINK "EASY RIDER" IS:

A) A CLASSIC MOVIE.

B) A PERSON WITH A MOTORCYCLE.

C) YOU, WHEN YOU REMEMBER TO TAKE THAT INFLATABLE PILLOW ON LONG CAR TRIPS.

"EASY RIDER"

BLOW

STORY PROBLEM

IF YOU THREW A BALL STRAIGHT UP IN THE AIR AND IT HIT THE GROUND 8 SECONDS LATER, HOW HIGH WOULD IT HAVE GONE, GIVEN THAT THE ACCELERATION OF GRAVITY IS 32 FEET PER SECOND?

ANSWER: TRICK QUESTION. YOU'D BE LUCKY TO LIFT YOUR ARM TO SHOULDER LEVEL, LET ALONE THROW A BALL.

YOU THINK OF "**THE TWIST**" AS:

A) A DANCE THAT WAS POPULAR IN YOUR YOUTH.
B) SOMETHING TO PUT IN YOUR MARTINI.
C) THE BEST WAY TO GET INTO YOUR JEANS.

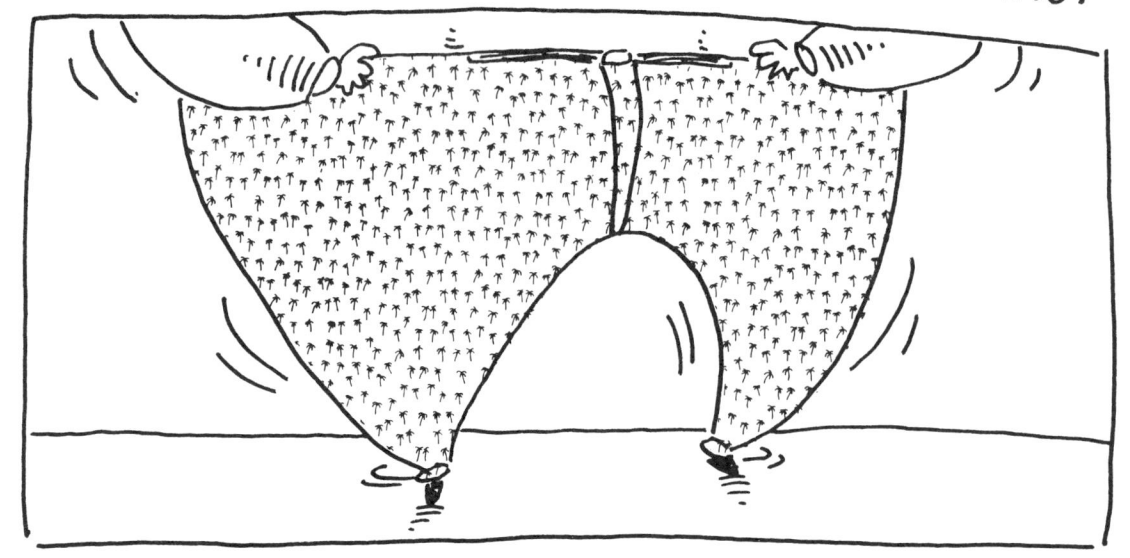

MATCH THE QUOTES ON THE LEFT WITH THE TITLES ON THE RIGHT.

1. "Call me Ishmael."

2. "A rose by any other name would smell as sweet."

3. "Frankly, Scarlett, I don't give a damn."

4. "Don't make any long-range plans."

A. Romeo and Juliet.

B. Moby Dick.

C. Your horoscope.

D. Gone With the Wind.

WEARING PANTS THAT ARE FAR TOO TIGHT IN THE SEAT IS:

A) AN AFFRONT TO POLITE SOCIETY.

B) SORT OF A PERSONAL TRADEMARK.

C) KINDA FUN!

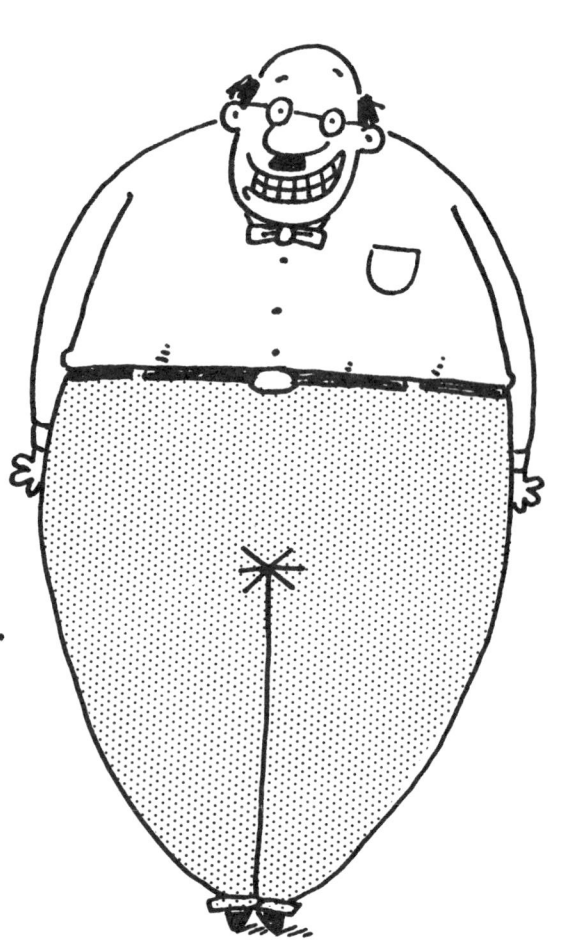

YOUR IDEA OF MUSIC TO MAKE LOVE BY IS:

A) "Bolero."

B) "The 1812 Overture."

C) "The Impossible Dream."

WHAT IS THIS PICTURE?

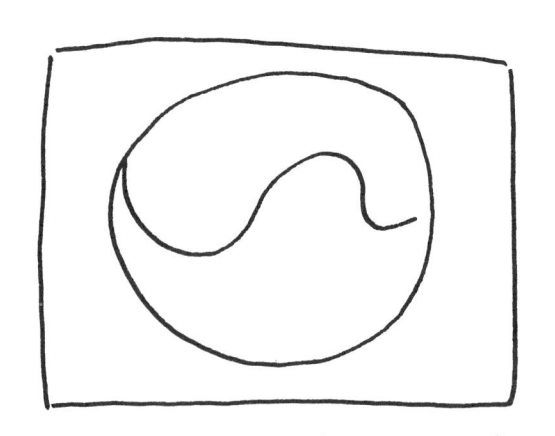

A) UNIVERSAL YIN AND YANG SYMBOL.
B) UNFINISHED SOFTBALL.
C) OVERHEAD VIEW OF HAIR CLEVERLY COMBED OVER BALD SPOT.

YOU ARE DOING YARD WORK WITH YOUR SHIRT OFF, THESE ARE THE FIRST WORDS YOU HEAR:

A) "How's the lawn doing?"
B) "Some weather we're having."
C) "You are under arrest."

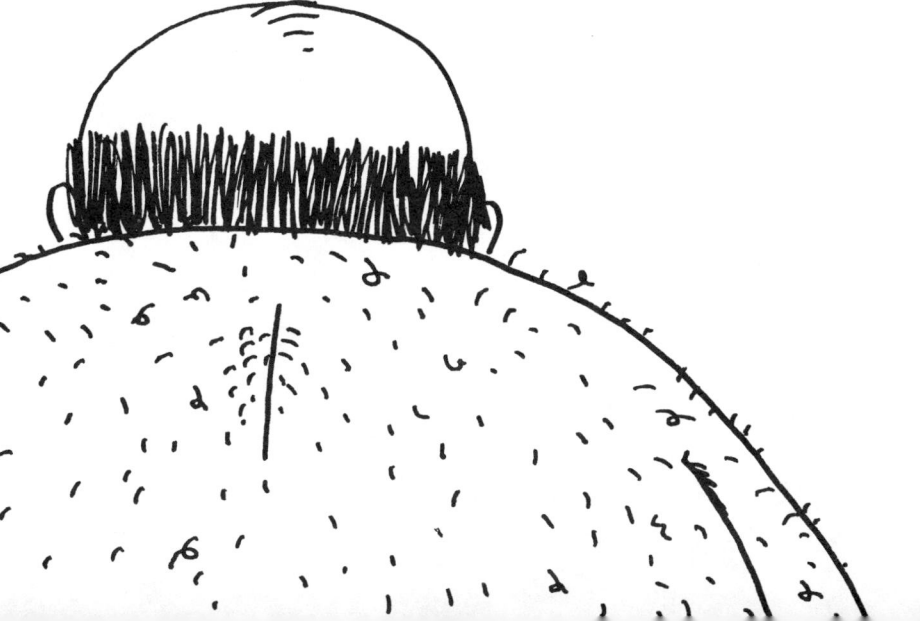

YOUR SEX LIFE IS:

A) THE ENVY OF YOUNG GUYS EVERYWHERE.

B) WILD, IMPETUOUS AND EXHAUSTING.

C) A VAGUE AND DISTANT MEMORY.